Mrs. Mayo's

How to Make

A

Wedding Cake

Written and Illustrated

by

ESTHER MURPHY

Mrs. Mayo's

How to Make a Wedding Cake

Copyright (C) 1980 Deco-Press Publishing Co.
First Printing   Nov. 1980
Second Printing   March 1981
Third Printing   October 1982
Fourth Printing   March 1987
Fifth Printing   Feb. 1992
Printed in the United States of America
Published By
DECO-PRESS/Mrs. Mayo's Co.
5660 Olde Wadsworth Blvd.
Denver (Arvada) Colo. 80002

ISBN 0-937016-00-4

Table of Contents

Foreward

Whether you're a professional retail baker/decorator or one who's been turning out party & special occasion cakes and now wants to do Wedding Cakes---this book is for you!

While there have been numerous books over the years devoted to "decorating" Wedding Cakes---this is the FIRST one to concern itself solely with "constructing" a cake, which is quite an art in itself.

You will find a gold mine of information here.

Not only do we tell you how to tier and separate cakes, but provide you with some superb recipes, new ideas, the yields of various size cake pans...and for the first time anywhere, we have figured the amount of icing you'll need to make any size cake!

While the retail baker/decorator will have his own mass production recipes, of course, the ones included here can be converted with ease to larger amounts.

Heretofore, the information contained in this book had to be culled from more than one source....a time consuming, frustrating and laborious process. And very often, not successful.

The one area we do not concern ourselves with is "decorating the cake". There are many excellent and colorfully illustrated books telling you "how to decorate" (some of them are listed in the back of this publication). This book is directed towards the person with some knowledge of decorating---but with little or no experience in constructing a Wedding Cake.

Even if you have done many Wedding Cakes, we feel you'll find new, time-saving tips here. The outstanding decorator is the one who believes you're never too old, or too young or too smart to learn something new. This person does not close their mind to improvement.

For the beginner, this book will take you from the breaking of the first egg for the batter through the completed cake on the reception table. The professional decorator experienced in baking & icing may want to go right to the nitty-gritty of assembling the cake.

The baker/decorator just going into business also will find many hints and secrets about producing Wedding Cakes for profit. And even established decorators may discover some help in this regard.

Turning out a stunning Wedding Cake can be as creative a challenge as one can imagine. It not only is emotionally fulfilling, but financially rewarding as well.

So....READ ON.... and HAPPY WEDDINGS!

The Publisher

ODE TO A WEDDING CAKE

I

Ode to a Wedding Cake

Creating a beautiful multi-tiered wedding cake can be as great a thrill for the cake decorator as it is for the bride when she sees it. Whether the cake is five feet tall or one foot or six tiers or two, making and decorating it is not much different than producing several one-tiered birthday cakes. Yet, for strange and unknown reasons, creating a wedding cake often causes decorators to lose all perspective!

A person who normally wouldn't dream of over-decorating a simple birthday cake will go off in a hundred different directions when planning a wedding cake. They place every kind of decoration, utilize every technique, and load the cake down with every conceivable plastic item imaginable! And the finished product is a gosh-awful, dreadfully over-decorated glob of baked goods.

In Wedding Cakes, as in anything else creative, the Decorator's watchword must be ...Restraint! Hold back when you have that mad desire to add more lattice work, or scrolls, extra bells, more cupids or flowers.

NUMBER OF GUESTS

First, the number of guests to be served will determine the size of the cake (included in this book are charts giving the number of servings each size cake will yield, as well as the amount of batter needed for producing the various sizes).

Secondly, you must have a design for the cake, so that any flowers or decorations can be made up in advance or purchased ahead of time. We can't stress enough the importance of making sure that everything is ready before starting out. This not only will reduce your labor time, but save you a great deal of frustration. Nothing can be more aggravating or potentially destructive to your work than having to stop in the middle of production because you don't have the right color or proper tip or correct size of separator plate, etc.

THE DESIGN

As for the cake design selected by the bride,(with your advice): In view of the many beautifully photographed books today, there is absolutely no reason to agonize over selecting a proper cake design. You can (1) design your own cake for the bride (2) choose one from a book and use it in its entirety, making only color changes as required or (3) combine several designs into one masterpiece.

PLAN AHEAD

Do as much baking and flower-making in advance as possible. Cakes can be frozen and, with meringue powder, you can make royal icing flowers that will last months in a dry area (if you use fresh egg whites for royal icing, you cannot make them up in advance because once the icing dries, it'll turn yellow).

If you wish a pure white cake and white icing, plan to use White Vanilla (sometimes called Clear Vanilla).

Planning ahead, therefore, makes cake decorating a joy---not a chore!

If improper planning (and that includes waiting to the last minute before starting to work) makes you stay up to 3 and 4 o'clock in the morning to get a cake out for a 9 o'clock delivery, you're going to be worn to a frazzle. And eventually, if that continues, you'll be "burned out". You simply won't enjoy what you've done, or what you have to do.

MATERIALS NEEDED

The following list of materials needed for the cake should be checked so everything will be ready:

a. Ingredients for cake and icing. (Recipes starting on Pages 29 & 48.)
b. Cake pans of proper sizes.
c. Paper for pan lining. (Brown wrapping paper, wax paper or parchment pan liners.)
d. Cake circles of proper sizes.

e. Heavy plate or three cake circles for base (4" wider than bottom tier).
f. Separators, plates, pegs and dowels for separated tiers.
g. Top ornament.
h. Tuk-n'-ruffle or doily. (See Page 83 for Tuk-n'ruffle needed.)
i. Coconut (See "Assembling the Tiers")

This illustration shows what is needed for a cake with separated tiers:

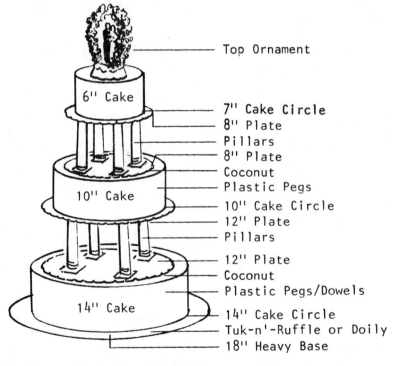

(For cake sizes other than the 6-10-14 shown, use the same procedure: Top tier has cake circle 1" larger than cake ((for bride to save)). All other tiers have same size cake circle. Each tier sets on plate 2" larger than tier. Plate on top of separator must be same size as plate on bottom.)

There should be at least 4" difference in diameters of tiers that are to be separated. For example, a 10" tier to be separated from a 14" tier beneath has to be set on a 12" plate and a 12" plate must be set on top of the 14" tier. Tiers with only 2" or 3" difference in diameters should be set directly on other tiers without separators between.

If tiers are not to be separated, the illustration below shows the materials needed:

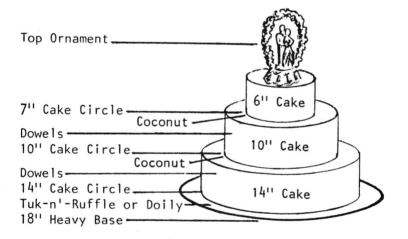

It is inadvisable to make more than a 3-tiered cake, if it is not to be separated, but will be transported. The three tiers, stacked together, may be part of a larger cake with additional tiers that will be transported separately.

SIZES and SERVINGS

II

Cake Sizes & Servings

(Based on a serving 1" x 2" x 2 layers high & cut by method shown on Pages 100 & 101)

ROUND TIERED CAKES

Servings	Size	Servings	Size
40	10-7	260	18-14-12-7 or 18-16-10-6
60	12-8		
100	12-10-7	290	18-14-12-9-7- or 20-26-10-7
120	14-10-7		
140	14-12-7	300	18-14-12-10-7
165	14-12-8-6	310	20-16-12-7
185	16-12-8-6	330	20-16-14-8
200	18-14-8	390	20-16-14-12-8
220	16-14-10-7	430	20-18-16-12-7
240	16-14-12-7	510	20-18-16-14-12-8

(The top tier is <u>not</u> included in the total number of servings listed above.)

Also, PLEASE NOTE: Round tiered cakes without separators cut by method shown on Pages 103 thru 105 yield a slightly different number of servings.

INDIVIDUAL TIERS

Heart	Square	Round	Servings
8".....	6"....	6".....	15
9".....	7"....	7".....	20
10".........	.....	8".....	25
	8"....	9".....	30
11".....	9".........	.....	35
12".........	......	10".....	40
	10".........	.....	50
14".........	......	12".....	60
	12".........	.....	70
16".........	......	14".....	80
18".....	14"....	16".....	100
20".....	16"....	18".....	120
22".....	18"....	20".....	150

(Petal & Hexagon Cake Servings slightly less than Round Cakes)

SHEET CAKES

Size	1-Layer *(2x2 pcs)*	2-Layers *(1x2 pcs)*
9" x 12"	24	54
9" x 13"	24	54
10" x 15"	35	75
11" x 15"	35	75
12" x 16"	48	96
12" x 18"	54	108
18" x 24"	96	216

MAKING THE BATTER

III

The All-Important Batter

Wedding cakes can be made from any good recipe that produces enough body and firmness enabling the shape to hold up under the added weight of icing and decorations when cakes are stacked in tiers. Traditionally, the bride's cake is white and the groom's cake is made of chocolate or dark fruitcake.

Whether you start from scratch or use a mix is entirely up to your personal preference. If you use a mix, please keep in mind that only two recipes can be successfully handled by a home mixer at one time.

We might suggest here that Hobart's KitchenAid K45 mixer is ideal for making cake batters & all types of icing. It has a double rotary action. Paddle revolves around bowl counter-clockwise while twirling clock-wise. Scrapes complete area within bowl. Sturdily built, it's the next best thing to a commercial mixer.

Although the volume of cake produced may vary slightly with different brands of cake mix, an average yield is 5 cups. The charts on Page 28 will help determine how many mixes are needed to make a particular size cake. If you prefer to mix your cakes from scratch, there are recipes following that have been tested and proven delicious to eat and, at the same time, firm enough to hold their shape when stacked up for wedding tiers.

While most prepared cake mixes are excellent, you may want to add something "extra" to make your cake a little bit different.

So, if you wish to use a mix instead of making a cake from scratch, here are some "doctoring up" tips. They apply to regular mixes, such as white, yellow and chocolate. In high altitudes, make sure to add the ingredients called for in the instructions on the box in addition to your own.

I don't suggest adding ingredients to mixes for Angel Food and Sponge Cakes (except those suggested for high altitude).

For a "Dream" Cake:

  Add 1 pkg. dry powdered Dream Whip
  2 extra eggs *(for yellow or chocolate cake)*

 or, the Dream Whip and
  2 egg whites *(for white cake mix)*

These should be added to the mix along with the ingredients listed on the box.

For a good-tastin' puddin' Cake:

    Add 1 pkg. instant Pudding Mix
    2 extra eggs *(2 egg whites only for white cake)*
    1/3 cup oil
    *(For chocolate cake, use chocolate pudding mix--
    for white or yellow cake, use vanilla pudding
    mix.)*

NOTE: Adding pudding works well in high altitudes but not so well at sea level. Some cake mixes have pudding included, and they work well at both sea level and high altitudes.

    Extra flavoring may be added to cake mixes if you wish to "perk up" the taste quality. Delete 1 teas. water from the amount needed for each teas. of flavoring added.

Suggestions:

    Add lemon flavoring to butter flavored yellow cake.

    Add <u>Creme Bouquet</u> *(See page 29)* to white cake mix.

    Add peppermint to devil's food or chocolate mix.

AMOUNT NEEDED

The amount of batter designated for the different sized pans is based upon the batter being placed in a pan to a thickness of approximately 1 1/8 inch. (Thickness will vary when the cake is baked, depending upon the type of batter used.)

All pans listed on the charts are 2" deep.

ROUND PANS

Size	Batter
6"....	1 1/4 cups
7"....	1 3/4 "
8"....	2 1/2 "
9"....	2 3/4 "
10"....	4 1/4 "
12"....	5 1/2 "
14"....	7 1/2 "
16"...	11 "
18"...	15 "
20"...	18 1/2 "

SQUARE PANS

Size	Batter
6"....	2 1/4 cups
7"....	3 1/2 "
8"....	4 "
9"....	5 1/2 "
10"....	7 "
12"...	10 "
14"...	14 "
16"...	19 1/2 "
18"...	24 "

RECTANGULAR PANS

Size	Batter
9" x 12"....	8 1/2 cups
9" x 13"....	10 "
10" x 15"....	12 "
11" x 15"....	13 "
12" x 16"....	14 "
12" x 18"....	16 "
18" x 24"....	32 "

Heart, Petal & Hexagon shaped pans require slightly less batter than Round Pans of comparable size.

RECIPES

BRIDE'S CAKE
(Wilton)

6 cups cake flour
  (+ 3 tbsp. for high altitude)
3 tbsp. baking powder
1 1/2 cups butter (3 sticks)
3 cups granulated sugar
2 1/2 cups milk
  (+ 1/4 cup for high altitude)
2 teas. clear white vanilla flavoring
1 1/8 cup egg whites (8 to 9 egg whites,
  depending on egg size)

Sift flour, measure & sift with baking
  powder three times.
Cream butter, gradually add sugar & continue
  creaming until light & fluffy.
Alternately add the flour mixture with milk
  and flavoring, beginning & ending with
  flour.
Fold in stiffly beaten egg whites.

Bake slightly longer than times listed on
  Baking Time Schedule. (See Pages 38 & 39)

Yield: 8 1/2 cups.

NOTE: There is a marvelous flavoring
      called "Creme Bouquet" that's great
      for wedding cakes. It's a blend of
      flavorings with a delicious vanilla-
      lemon taste.

      Available in 4 oz., 16 oz. & 1 gal. bottles.

WHITE WEDDING CAKE
(Good Housekeeping)

7 1/2 cups sifted cake flour
  (+ 3 1/2 tbsp. for high altitude)
8 1/2 teas. baking powder
2 teas. salt
1 2/3 cups shortening
4 cups granulated sugar
2 1/2 cups milk
  (+ 1/4 cup for high altitude)
12 egg whites
1/3 cup granulated sugar
2 teas. Creme Bouquet flavoring

1. Sift flour with baking powder & salt.
   Prepare pans with liners.
   Start heating oven to 350°F.

2. In a large bowl with mixer at medium speed,
   cream shortening while gradually adding
   4 cups granulated sugar until very light
   & fluffy; transfer mixture to 8-qt. pan.

   Alternately mix in flour mixture and milk,
   starting and ending with flour mixture.
   Add flavoring with the milk.

3. In a large bowl, with mixer at high speed,
   or with wire whip, beat egg whites until
   they foam, then gradually beat in 1/3 cup
   granulated sugar until mixture is stiff.
   Fold into batter.

4. Bake according to times listed on Baking
   Time Schedule. (See Pages 38 & 39)

(Yield: 14 cups)

GROOM'S CHOCOLATE CAKE

3 oz. chocolate, melted (3 squares)*
1 cup butter
2 cups granulated sugar

* *(To substitute cocoa:*
    3 level tbsp. cocoa + 1 tbsp. vegetable oil,
      mixed together, = 1 square of chocolate.

5 eggs, unbeaten
1 teas. baking soda
1 cup buttermilk
2 1/2 cups cake flour, sifted
1/2 teas. salt
2 teas. vanilla flavoring

1. Melt chocolate over simmering water. Cool.
2. Cream butter with sugar until light & fluffy.
3. Add eggs one at a time. Beat well after each addition. Blend in melted chocolate (or cocoa & oil).
4. Dissolve soda in buttermilk.
5. Sift flour once before measuring.
6. Mix & sift flour & salt together.
7. Add dry ingredients alternately with buttermilk, mixing thoroughly after each addition.
8. Add vanilla. Mix well.

    Bake slightly longer than times listed on Baking Time Schedule. (See Pages 38 & 39)

(Yield: 7 cups)

32

ADJUSTING CAKE BATTERS FOR HIGH ALTITUDES

To convert low altitude cake recipes for use at altitudes 4,000 to 6,000 feet, the following ingredient changes are recommended:

1. For each cup of flour in recipe, add 2 level teaspoons.

2. For each 1,000 feet rise in altitude, decrease sugar in recipe, 1/2 tablespoon per cup called for.

3. For each 1,000 feet rise in altitude, decrease shortening in recipe, 1/2 teaspoon per cup called for.

4. Decrease 1/4 to 1/2 teaspoon baking powder, soda or cream of tartar from recipe.

5. Add 2 to 3 tablespoons liquid per cup called for in recipe.

NOTE: Try smaller adjustment first if two amounts are given.

BAKING

IV

It's Time for Baking

Women used to be judged as to how good a cook they were by their cakes, especially when the cakes were shown (and sampled) at county fairs, bazaars, harvest time, etc. Nowadays, with more & more women doing special occasion cakes at home, they are more likely to be judged as to how good a baker they are.

Baking a wedding cake correctly is just as important as knowing how to put it together and decorate it. No matter how beautiful the cake may be on the outside, if it is too porous (lots of big holes) or soggy (too moist and heavy) on the inside, it probably hasn't been baked right. If it has a fine texture (no holes) and is not soggy, it'll be a much better eating - and looking - cake.

Even if you haven't baked a large cake before, there's nothing to be afraid of. If you have plenty of time before the cake is needed, bake the cakes when you are in a creative mood and freeze them. *(Paragraph 7)*

TIPS FOR SUCCESSFUL BAKING

The following suggestions may help in the successful baking of wedding cakes:

1. Trace around cake pan on brown wrapping or wax paper. Cut inside of tracing line.

2. Grease sides and bottom of pan with shortening (do not use liquid oil - makes cakes stick). Press paper down in bottom of pan. Pan Coating can be used instead of shortening.

3. For pans of unusual shapes which cannot satisfactorily be lined with paper on bottom, use Pan Coating, or grease with shortening and dust with flour.

4. Do not use more than 1 1/4" of batter in a pan regardless of how deep the pan may be. It is better to have thinner layers. They are easier to handle.

5. Using a spatula, push the batter up evenly around the sides of the pan, making the center lower. This helps keep the cake level when it is baked.

   One method for preventing a hump rising on the cake while baking: Cut terry cloth (from old towels) into two inch strips, dampen, then pin double strip around cake pan with safety pin. Do not overlap. Strips should not be any wider than depth of pan.

6. Cover any cake batter that you're unable to bake immediately and place in refrigerator.

7. Cakes can be baked several weeks ahead, then frozen. <u>Cool</u> <u>cakes</u> <u>completely</u>, wrap in plastic wrap (airtight), then place in freezer. Defrost at room temperature. <u>Do</u> <u>not</u> place in oven to defrost.

8. Cakes already iced and decorated can be frozen several weeks ahead. Wrapping not necessary (icing keeps cakes moist). Remove from freezer <u>at</u> <u>least</u> <u>12</u> <u>hours</u> before cutting.

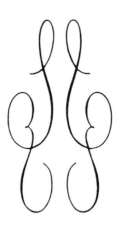

BAKING TIMES

The baking times listed in the following charts are approximate, since the consistency of the batter may vary in different cake recipes. Some cake batters are light and airy and should be baked at the normally listed baking times, whereas, others are heavier (similar to pound cakes) and should be baked slightly longer than normal.

Probably the best method for judging when the cake is done is by piercing it in the center with a cake tester or toothpick. If tester is clean when withdrawn, cake is done. If batter clings to tester, cake requires more baking.

PLEASE NOTE: If you are using a cake mix, disregard instructions on side of box for high altitude baking. Temperature suggested is much too high. Use the instructions for high altitude baking following these charts.

BAKING TIME & TEMPERATURE SCHEDULE

ROUND PANS

Size	Bake Times	Temp.
6"	25-30 min	350°F.
7"	25-30 "	"
8"	30-35 "	"
9"	30-35 "	"
10"	35-40 "	"
12"	40-45 "	"

14"- 16"- 18"- 20"...Bake 45 min. plus additional time at 350°F. until done.

SQUARE PANS

Size	Bake Times	Temp.
6".......	30-35 min.......	350°F.
7".......	30-35 "	"
8".......	35-40 "	"
9".......	35-40 "	"
10".......	40-45 "	"
12".......	45-50 "	"

14"-16"-18"...Bake 45 min. plus
additional time at 350° until done.

RECTANGULAR PANS

Size	Bake Times	Temp.
9" x 12"...	40-45 min........	350°F.
9" x 13"...	40-45 "	"
10" x 15"...	45-55 "	"
11" x 15"...	45-55 "	"
12" x 16"...	45-55 "	"

12" x 18") Bake 50 min. plus addi-
18" x 24") tional time at 350° until
done.

For Heart, Petal & Hexagon shaped pans, use
the chart for Round Pans.

HIGH ALTITUDE BAKING

After many years of extensive tests on
baking cakes in high altitudes, we have come
to the conclusion that there is very little,
if any, adjustment necessary in the oven
temperature from that used in a low altitude.
The difference in making cakes in high
altitudes is in the adjustment of ingredients, rather then the baking.

The recommended temperature of 375°F.
for high altitude baking of cake mixes is
much too high. We suggest preheating the
oven to 350° for either a low or high altitude.

DUMPING

V

Dumping the Cake

1. Cool in pan on rack for at least 10 min. (15 to 20 min. for 14" or larger).

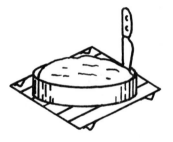

2. Use sharp knife in up & down movement to loosen sides.

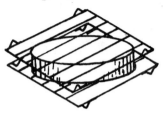

3. Place another rack or cardboard over cake in pan. Turn over so cake is bottomside up.

4. Remove top rack. Dump cake from pan.

5. Replace top rack. Turn cake over again so cake is <u>right side up</u>.

6. Remove top rack. Let cake cool <u>completely</u>. Refrigerate or freeze layers.

MAKING THE ICING

VI

The Icing - and How to Make It

(Part 1)

Icing should enhance the flavor of a cake as well as making a good looking background for your decorations. Creme Bouquet or Clear White Vanilla flavoring in the icing will complement almost any flavored cake (including chocolate) and will keep the icing white.

The correct consistency of icing also is important because it must spread easily over the cake for maximum smoothness. If you test the icing before applying to the cake and it seems too stiff or heavy to spread, add a little extra liquid to the recipe.

BUTTERCREAM ICING (For icing cakes)

1/2 cup + 2 tbsp. Crisco
1 lb. powdered sugar
    (3 3/4 cups unsifted or 4 cups sifted)
1/8 cup powdered·non-dairy cream
    (coffee cream)
1/2 teas. salt
1/3 cup water
1 teas. Creme Bouquet or Clear White Van-
    illa flavoring
2 drops only butter flavoring

With mixer at low speed, mix powdered sugar,
Crisco, salt & powdered cream until smooth.

Gradually add combined water & flavoring at
slow speed, then beat at medium speed until
fluffy, smooth and of spreading consistency.

                    (Yield: 3 3/4 cups)
*(This buttercream can also be used for making bor-
ders but is not recommended for making flowers,
such as roses, chrysanthemums, etc.)*

BUTTERCREAM ICING (For decorating only)

1 1/4 cup Crisco
1 lb. powdered sugar
3 tbsp. water
1 teas. Clear White Vanilla or Creme Bouquet
2 drops only butter flavoring
1/16 teas. salt

Whip Crisco at high speed until fluffy.
Add 1/2 of the powdered sugar. Mix at low
    speed until blended.
Add water & flavoring. Mix at medium speed
    until thoroughly blended.
Add balance of powdered sugar, then whip at
    high speed until fluffy.

CHOCOLATE BUTTERCREAM ICING (For icing cakes*)

1/3 cup Crisco
1/3 cup butter or margarine
3/4 cup cocoa (packed down)
1/2 cup milk
1 lb. powdered sugar
1 tbsp. white Karo
1 teas. vanilla flavoring
1/8 teas. salt

Cream butter & Crisco together.
Blend cocoa into creamed mixture.
Add milk slowly and blend.
Add powdered sugar slowly and blend.
Add vanilla, Karo, salt &
    1 teas. liquid brown coloring
    1/8 teas.   "   black   "
    1/8 teas.   "   red   "

Blend, then whip at high speed until fluffy.

(Yield: 3 1/2 cups)

*For decorating cake - borders, roses, etc.:

Add 2 cups powdered sugar & blend. Whip at high
speed until fluffy.

(Yield: 4 cups)

ROYAL ICING (made with Meringue Powder)
(For making flowers & decorations ahead)

1 lb. powdered sugar
1/4 cup meringue powder *(available at Mrs. Mayo's)*
1/2 cup tap water
1/8 teas. cream of tartar

Dry mix sugar, meringue powder &
    cream of tartar.
Add water & blend.
Whip at high speed until stands in high peak
    on spatula. (8 to 15 minutes, depending
    on mixer*)

Keep well covered at all times with damp
    cloth or airtight cover. Dries very
    fast. Also, utensils must be grease
    free. *(Grease makes this icing break down)*
    Do not refrigerate. Can be kept at
    room temperature for several weeks,
    then re-whipped and used again.

                (Yield: 3 1/2 cups)

* *If you are using an electric mixer other than a
KitchenAid or other heavy duty upright mixer, we
recommend that you make only one-half batch of
royal at a time.*

ROYAL ICING (made with powdered egg whites)

1 lb. powdered sugar
2 tbsp. powdered egg whites
1/2 teas. cream of tartar
1/3 cup tap water

Mix by same method as above, substituting
    powdered egg whites for meringue powder
    and changing amounts of ingredients as
    printed in this recipe.

Same rules apply - no grease - keep airtight, etc.

ROYAL ICING (made with fresh egg whites)

1 lb. powdered sugar (4 cups sifted)
3 egg whites (med. size eggs)
      at room temperature.
1/2 teas. cream of tartar

Blend ingredients, then whip at high speed
      8 to 15 minutes, depending on mixer.

Use same procedure as for other royal icing
      recipes - no grease - keep airtight,etc.

This icing with fresh egg whites must be
      used immediately and cannot be re-
      whipped.

                    (Yield: 2 1/2 cups)

VII

The Icing - and How Much

You Need

(Part 2)

Various types of buttercream may yield slightly different amounts, depending on whether the icing is light and fluffy, or heavy. This depends upon the recipe and your mixer. The amounts in the following charts are based on an average yield of 3 3/4 cups per batch of icing made with 1 lb. of powdered sugar.

Amounts of icing for the different sized cakes are listed in cups & tablespoons. This gives you a basis for figuring how many batches will be needed to ice and decorate a particular size cake. For example, a 9" round cake would require 2 1/2 cups to ice and 1 cup to decorate. Therefore, 1 batch would be sufficient. A 14-10-6 tiered cake would require 10 cups to ice and 3 1/4 cups to decorate---a total of 13 1/4 cups. Four recipes would yield 15 cups, which should be sufficient.

54

The required amounts listed on the charts are based on round & square cakes being 2 layers, approximately 3" deep and the icing being approximately 1/8" thick.* Icing needed for decorating is based on using a #32 shell border around base, a #16 shell border around top edge and #16 tube scalloped garland around sides. The icing listed for decorating the cakes <u>does</u> <u>not</u> <u>include</u> <u>any</u> <u>flowers</u> <u>or</u> <u>leaves</u>.

Petal cakes require slightly more icing than round cakes of the same size. Heart & Hexagon cakes require slightly less. The chart of Sheet cakes lists icing needed for 1-layer (1 1/2" deep) and 2-layer (3" deep).

*If a coating thicker than 1/8" is preferred, simply make more icing than the amounts listed.

This basic chart will help in figuring the amount of icing needed:

          2 tbsp.= 1/8 cup
          4 tbsp.= 1/4 cup
          8 tbsp.= 1/2 cup
         12 tbsp.= 3/4 cup
         16 tbsp.= 1 cup

ROUND CAKES

SIZE (2-layer)	TO ICE CAKE: (Incl.filling)	TO DECORATE:
6".....	1 1/2 cups.....	10 tbsp.
7".....	1 3/4 "	13 tbsp.
8".....	2 1/4 "	15 tbsp.
9".....	2 1/2 "	1 cup
10".....	3 1/4 "	1 cup + 2 tbsp.
12".....	4 "	1 cup + 5 tbsp.
14".....	5 1/4 "	1 1/2 cups
16".....	6 1/2 "	1 3/4 cups
18".....	8 "	2 cups
20".....	9 1/2 "	2 1/4 cups

SQUARE CAKES

SIZE (2-layer)	TO ICE CAKE: (Incl.filling)	TO DECORATE:
6".....	2 cups.....	14 tbsp.
7".....	2 1/2 "	1 cup + 1 tbsp.
8".....	2 3/4 "	1 1/4 cups
9".....	3 1/4 "	1 cup + 5 tbsp.
10".....	4 "	1 1/2 cups
12".....	5 1/4 "	1 3/4 cups
14".....	6 3/4 "	2 cups
16".....	8 1/4 "	2 1/4 cups
18".....	10 cups.........	2 1/2 cups

SHEET CAKES
(One Layer)

SIZE	TO ICE CAKE:	TO DECORATE: *(No garland)*
9" x 12"..	2 cups..........	1 cup
9" x 13"..	2 cups+2 tbsp...	1 cup+1 tbsp.
10" x 15"..	2 cups+9 tbsp...	1 cup+3 tbsp.
11" x 15"..	2 3/4 cups......	1 1/4 cups
12" x 16"..	3 cups+2 tbsp...	1 cup+6 tbsp.
12" x 18"..	3 1/2 cups......	1 1/2 cups
18" x 24"..	6 1/4 cups......	2 cups

SHEET CAKES
(Two Layer)

SIZE	TO ICE CAKE: *(Incl.filling)*	TO DECORATE: *(W/garland)*
9" x 12"..	3 3/4 cups......	1 1/2 cups
9" x 13"..	4 cups..........	1 1/2 cups
10" x 15"..	5 cups..........	1 3/4 cups
11" x 15"..	5 1/2 cups......	2 cups
12" x 16"..	6 cups+2 tbsp...	2 cups
12" x 18"..	6 3/4 cups......	2 cups+3 tbsp.
18" x 24"..	12 cups.........	3 1/4 cups

ICING THE CAKE

VIII

Icing the Cake

All tiers of the cake are to be iced separately, then assembled. This applies to separated tiers and stacked tiers. Each tier is iced on a cake circle same size as cake. Ice all tiers before assembling them.

1. Trim off any humps or uneven portions of cake top by using a back & forth movement with a serrated knife. Cake must be absolutely even on all sides & center.

2. Smear icing on cake circle. Place this upsidedown on cake top and turn cake over. Cake is bottomsideup on cake circle.

   Peel off lining paper & trim cake if any burned spots. *(It is not necessary to trim layer if only nicely browned around sides and bottom.)*

3. Spread filling on layer. Place second layer on top, bottom side up. *(All cake layers are set in place on tiers, <u>bottomsideup</u>.)* If layer is 14" or larger, may be necessary to slide it off a cardboard or cookie sheet onto bottom layer, rather than picking it up as can be done with 12" or smaller.

If a fruit or custard filling is desired, use a #12 tube and buttercream icing and pipe a "fence" all around the edge of the cake, then spread the filling inside this. Do not make the filling too thick. (May ooze out through icing or make top layer slide.)

To make a richer tasting cake, layers can be sliced in two, making four layers and three fillings. Makes cake more moist also.

After layers are filled, spread a very thin coat of icing over the entire cake, by scraping the icing over cake surface with spatula. *(Excess icing scraped off the cake should not be returned to icing bowl. Contains crumbs.)* This is called "crumbing" the cake and will prevent any loose crumbs from getting into the outer coat of icing.

4. Before applying icing to cake, be sure it is free of air bubbles. To do this, use straight from mixer, or stir vigorously with spatula.

Place cake on turn table or stand. Spread icing over top of cake, pushing excess down over sides, then apply dabs of icing around sides to cover.

5. Use long strokes with spatula to make sides, then top, as smooth as possible. This is where a turn table is almost essential. The combination of long strokes with the spatula and turning the table makes it much easier to make the icing smooth.

6. NOW, to obtain a <u>really</u> smooth, slick surface: Spray fine <u>mist</u> of water over top
   and sides. Scrape off excess water with
   spatula wiped on damp towel after each
   scraping. Dab damp cloth around base to
   remove any more excess water.

   This method works fine on white or a <u>very</u>
   <u>pale</u> colored buttercream. It should not
   be used on icing that is colored a deep-
   er shade. Makes white streaks on the
   icing surface.

ASSEMBLING TIERS

IX

Assembling Tiers

The most important things to remember when assembling cakes are that (1) each one must be as even as possible (not lopsided), (2) they must be set exactly in center of tiers underneath and (3) must be made as sturdy as possible (with pegs & dowels) so cake can be transported and set on reception table without collapsing. Don't let all this scare you...it's simply a matter of making each separate tier as neat as possible, then setting them together correctly to produce a cake that stands straight on the reception table.

Step 1. Place the bottom tier of the cake on a sturdy base at least 4" larger than the tier itself. Use either a heavy plastic base...or...one cut out of masonite or plywood for cakes larger than a 12"-10"-7". If using cardboard circles for base of larger cakes, use at least three circles, placed together so grains are crosswise and taped around the edge with scotch tape. (If base is flexible, icing will tend to crack.)

If using cardboard, masonite or plywood base, cover top, lapping over edges with florist's foil. Fasten underneath with scotch tape. This makes a prettier base. Tuk-n'-Ruffle or a doily can be used on top of the covered base. *(Florist's foil can be purchased at some cake decorating supply stores, hobby shops, etc.)*

If using doily, stick it to base with icing. Then, smear icing on top of doily, and set bottom tier in place.

If using Tuk-n'-Ruffle, smear icing on base, then set cake in place. Use scissors to cut narrow edge of ruffle off to about 1/8" from stitching. Pipe a line of icing around base of cake with a #12 tube, pushing the tube against the corner between the baseboard and base of cake. Press the narrow edge of ruffle down into the icing all around the cake. Bottom border will cover icing and edge of ruffle. On separated tiers, use doily or ruffle only on bottom tier.

If the second tier is to be set directly on the bottom tier <u>without</u> separators, push a 1/4" wooden dowel into the bottom tier 2" to 3" from the edge of the cake until it touches the base. Mark dowel at surface of icing. Lift dowel straight up. Cut it off at marking. (Use wire cutter or large pliers or place old knife on dowel and hit with hammer to cut through.) Push dowel back into cake again. Repeat until you have a circle of at least 5 to 7 dowels in the bottom tier.

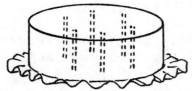

PLEASE NOTE: If the tiers are extra large & heavy, such as a 14"-12"-9"-7" setting on top of a 16" bottom, whether separated or not, the 16" tier should have 1/2" dowels, instead of 1/4". The 1/2" dowels have to be cut with a coping saw.

Step 2. Before setting the second tier down on the bottom one, sprinkle a small amount of coconut (macaroon or shredded) over the area where the second tier is to be placed. (This will prevent the icing from sticking to the cardboard under the second tier when it is removed for cutting.) Now, set the second tier down in the center of the bottom tier.

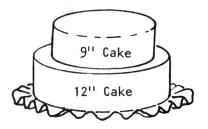

If the third tier is to be set directly on the second tier, proceed with placing dowels in the second tier as was done in the bottom tier, using fewer dowels on the smaller tier, but never less than 4. (If top tier is only 6", no need for dowels underneath.) Sprinkle coconut on second tier before placing third one on top.

TIERS WITH NO SEPARATORS BETWEEN must be decorated <u>after</u> they are assembled.

TIERS TO BE SEPARATED are usually decorated separately, then assembled at place of reception.

Step 3. When separators are placed between tiers, use the four plastic pegs that come with the plate, instead of wooden dowels, <u>unless</u> the tiers above the separators are extra large & heavy. In this case, use wooden dowels in addition to the four plastic pegs.

In any event, the larger & heavier the upper
tiers, the more dowels should be used in the
lower tiers. Use a wire cutter or heavy
kitchen shears to cut pegs to size.

Step 4. Before setting the plate on the
lower tier, snap the pegs onto underside,
press pegs lightly into surface of icing,
then remove. Measure spaces from each marking
out to edges of cake
to make sure the plate
will be centered. If
using extra dowels,
place them down into
the cake at this point,
then sprinkle coconut
over area to be
covered by plate.

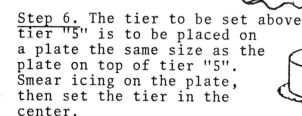

10" Plate

12" Cake

Step 5. Set plate in
place, pushing the
pegs down into cake.

Step 6. The tier to be set above
tier "5" is to be placed on
a plate the same size as the
plate on top of tier "5".
Smear icing on the plate,
then set the tier in the
center.

8" Cake

10" Plate

Step 7. If another tier is to
be separated above tier "6",
set a plate 2" larger than
the upper tier in the center
of tier "6", making sure the
legs on top and bottom
plates are exactly in line
vertically. Set the upper tier on the same
size plate as is on top of tier "7".

Step 8. When the cake is
assembled, the separa-
tors should be lined up
vertically on all tiers.
*(Although the separated tiers
are usually decorated separately, then assembled,
it's a good idea to test
the vertical line-up by
putting the tiers to-
gether before deco-
rating.*

Then, disassemble to decorate.)

USING OTHER TYPES OF CAKE SEPARATORS

LACE CAKE STAND

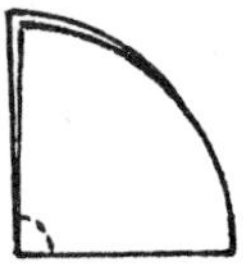

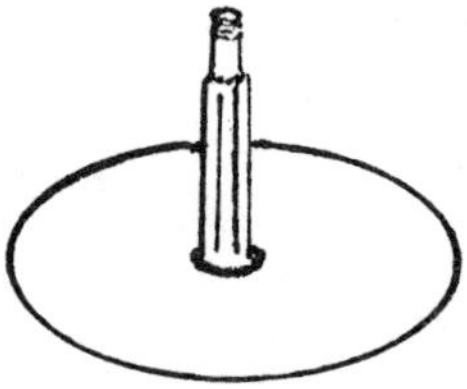

Step 1. When using this cake
stand, each tier, as well as
the cake circle underneath,
must have a hole cut in the
center. Trace around the cake
circles on paper, cut the
paper circles out, then
fold over twice. Cut off
the corner fold about 3/4".
Test the holes over the
lower portion of a center
column to see if large
enough.

Place each paper on its same size cake
circle and mark around the holes, then cut
out with a sharp pointed knife.

Step 2. Smear icing on the circles then set
each tier on its appropriate circle. Use
the same paper circles with holes cut out
to mark each tier except the top one. Use
a cake corer or long thin sharp knife to
cut holes out of the lower tiers. Then,
ice the tiers.

The lace cake stand includes six plates,
18"-16"-14"-12"-10"-8". Illustrated here
are three plates, 18"-14"-10", holding three
cake tiers, 16"-12"-8". If a smaller cake
is desired, glue-on legs are available to
use on the smaller plates.*

* If using the 16" plate (or smaller) for the base,
glue only three legs on the plate. Screw the column
in tightly, then screw the Four-Arm Nut underneath.
(The bottom column bolt used on the 18" base plate
is too tall for the smaller plates.) .

Step 3. The tiers may be assembled on the plates and columns and decorated, or may be decorated separately on plates. To do the latter, place each plate in a cake pan 2" smaller than plate. For example, set the 14" plate with the 12" tier in a 12" cake pan to keep steady while it is being decorated. The base plate will not need the cake pan since it has legs. However, before setting the cake tier on the base plate, screw the column into the plate, then the bottom column bolt (or the Four-Arm Nut for smaller cake) underneath. The tier can then be eased down over the column and set in place.

Step 4. To assemble the whole cake, first, screw the bottom column bolt underneath. Set the 16" tier straight down over the column onto the 18" base plate. Set the 14" plate on the column.

16" Cake
on 18" Plate

Step 5. Set the 12" tier down on the 14" plate, then insert column & screw tightly to secure. Set the 10" plate on the column and screw top cap nut on tightly.

12" Cake
on 14" Plate

Step 6. Set the 8" tier
on the 10" plate. Cake
can now be decorated,
then disassembled for
delivery.   Deliver
tiers separately by
setting the upper
tiers in cake pans
2" smaller than
plates.Base plate
with legs can be
set on foam rubber
sheet for delivery.
(See Page 92 on
Delivering the Cakes.)

8" Cake on
10" Plate

12" Cake
on 14" Plate

16" Cake
on 18" Plate

4-ARM SUPPORT ATTACHMENT
FOR LACE·CAKE STAND

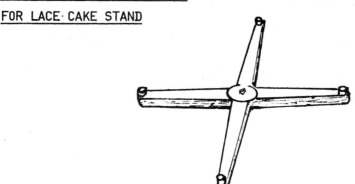

If a cake is needed larger than the Lace Cake Stand will hold, replace the 18" base with the 4-Arm Support Attachment. Four plates (10" or 12") can be used to add extra servings and will give an airy look to the tall stand.

It is not necessary to cut holes in the cake circles used on these plates.

Smear icing on the four plates, set the tiers on them and decorate.

Insert the 4-Arm Base Nut underneath the Support Attachment, then screw a 7½" column on top.

Cake tiers on plates can now be set on the 4 arms and the upper tiers assembled as before, using the 6½" columns.

6" Cake
8" Plate

14" Cake

16" Plate

8" Cake

10" Plate

CRYSTAL CLEAR DIVIDER STAND

This type cake stand has clear plastic dividers that go right through the cake. The set includes six plates: 16"-14"-12"-10"-8"-6". Illustrated here is an 18" baseboard with 14" cake tier, 12" plate with 10" cake tier and an 8" plate with 6" cake tier.

Step 1. To use this type divider stand, ice the tiers as before, each on a cake circle same size as the tier.

Step 2. Smear icing on a sturdy 18" baseboard and set the 14" tier on this. Set a 12" plate down lightly in the center of the 14" tier so as to leave markings in the four spots where the dividers will be placed in the tier. Remove the plate and carefully push the dividers straight down into the tier until they rest on the baseboard.

14" Cake on 18" Base

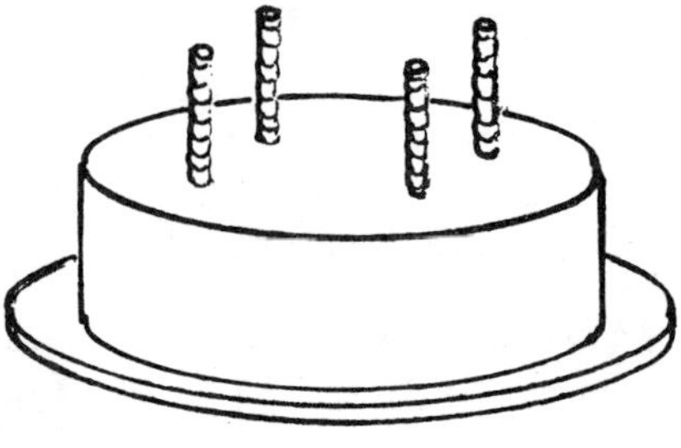

Step 3. Set the 10" tier down in the center of the 12" plate, sticking it on as before. Set the 8" plate down lightly in the center of the 10" tier, making markings for dividers.

10" Cake on 12" Plate

IMPORTANT: The plate should be placed so the markings on the cake top will be in line with the divider holders underneath the 12" plate the tier is setting on. Remove the 8" plate.

Step 4. Push the dividers down into the 10"
tier and stick the 6" tier down on the 8"
plate.

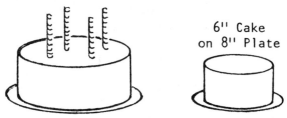

6" Cake
on 8" Plate

Step 5. Set the 6" tier on the dividers and
the cake is ready to be decorated.

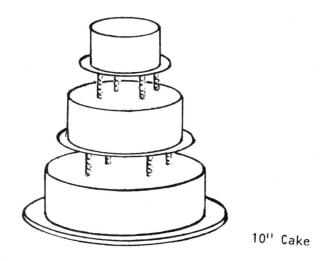

10" Cake

NOTE: *This type tiered cake may be decorated before
the tiers are assembled or after assembly.
In either case, the tiers are to be transported separately, then assembled at place
of reception.*

ASSEMBLING A FOUNTAIN CAKE

There's nothing like a fountain to enhance the beauty of a wedding cake. The cake
has to be a rather large size to accommodate
the fountain between two tiers. 14" plates
are the minimum size on which a fountain will
fit, so a 16" or 18" tier would be used underneath and a 12" tier on top, then smaller tiers
on the 12" if desired. Also, the pillars used
with a fountain must be at least 10" or taller.
*(When using 10" pillars, the top cascade must be
left off the fountain.)*

The 13" Arched Pillars and the 12" Lacy-
Look Pillars are ideal for use with a fountain.

The 13" Arched Pillars are generally used
in sets of six between 18" plates as illustrated
below. Real or artificial flowers or greenery
can be placed around the fountain base at time
of assembly. Set the fountain in the center of
the plate, set the pillars in place, then
the flowers or greenery.

*(Instructions
come with the
fountain in re-
gards to putting
the water in,
coloring the
water, etc.)*

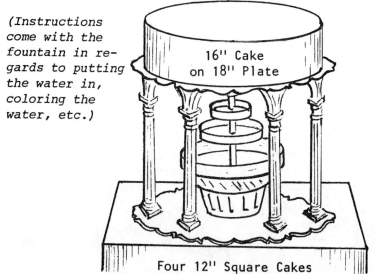

16" Cake
on 18" Plate

Four 12" Square Cakes

Use the Lacy-Look Pillars on a 14" plate
or larger, as illustrated below. Again, the
fountain is set on the plate at the time of
assembly, then the pillars, & finally, flowers
or greenery around the fountain base.

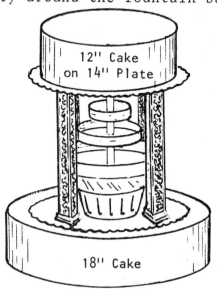

As an alternative to using the fountain
between tiers of a wedding cake, it can also
be used as the top tier
by enclosing it in a
12" styrofoam shell,
using the following
method...

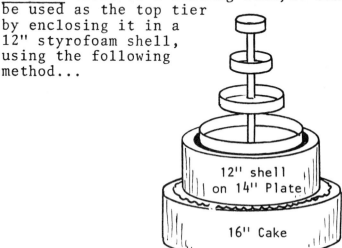

To make the shell, cut circle, 10" in diameter, from a 12" styrofoam cake dummy, 4" high. Cut a small indentation at the bottom rim of the shell for the electric cord to run under. Line shell with foil and set on a 14" plate. Ice sides and top rim with royal, then use royal to pipe border and decorations just as you would on a real cake tier.

The cake tier underneath has to be 16" with a 14" plate on top. When assembling the whole cake, set the decorated shell on the divider columns, then place the fountain inside.

AS A CENTERPIECE

The fountain can also be used as a centerpiece, or two fountains can be used on the table, one on either side of the wedding cake. Make a shell for the fountain as before, setting it on a 14" base, icing and decorating it in royal. The fountain(s) can be set directly on the table and does not have to have flowers or greenery surrounding it.

PLACING DECORATIONS

PRACTICE TARGET

X

Decorations

– and How to Place Them

There are hundreds of cake decorating books on the market, most of them excellent. If you've been doing cakes very long, you probably have a sizeable library of these books. And like any good library, the books should be used for researching ideas, techniques, and designs.

If you can't think of a good design, make use of those in the various books.

Don't be afraid to use, or adapt, a design from another source. After all, that's why books are published--to use!

You may use ideas from these books as a whole, or in connection with your own special skills in creating a masterpiece.

There are some decorators so honest that they refuse to use book ideas, feeling ---erroneously---that they would be violating the copyright, or that to do so, they would be "stealing".

On the contrary, books were published for the "use" of decorators.

PLANNING A DESIGN

Although this book's purpose is not to
teach "how to decorate" a cake, here are
some basic suggestions that may help you in
the placement of decorations when you are
creating your own designs.

1.   In planning a design, select a theme
and carry it throughout the entire cake.
For example, if you are using roses and lil-
ies of the valley, these same flowers should
be used on every tier that is to have flowers. Borders may be alternated on the tiers,
but should be similar in design. Also, the
borders and side garlands should be predom-
inately white. If color is used, it should
match the color of the flowers, and be used
very sparingly.

2.   TIERS WITH SEPARATORS can easily be
divided into equal spaces for placement of
flower sprays and/or side garlands and decorations simply by placing same at each separator and/or halfway between. For very
large cakes, the spaces between separators
may be divided into three or four spaces
instead of just two.

3.   TO DIVIDE TIERS WITHOUT SEPARATORS into
equal spaces around the cake, multiply the
diameter of the cake by 3.1416. This will
give you the distance around the cake.* For
example, a 14" diameter cake, multiplied by
3.1416 equals approximately 44". To get 12
equal spaces around the cake, divide 44 by
12, which would give you 12 spaces, each of
them 2 2/3" long. 8 spaces around a 14"
cake would each be 5 1/2" long. Use toothpick to mark spaces on cake edge.

*The distance around the bottom tier will also give
you the correct length of Tuk-n'-Ruffle needed.

4. TO MAKE SAME SIZE GARLANDS in between markings, use a Garland Marker...or...use round plastic lid or cardboard circle to make a slight imprint in each space. Circle width is determined by width of spaces. Depth of scalloped garland is determined by how far down on the cake side the circle is placed.

5. Sprays of flowers or decorations on tiered cakes may be:

(a) placed at the same marking on each tier

OR

(b) placed between markings on every other tier

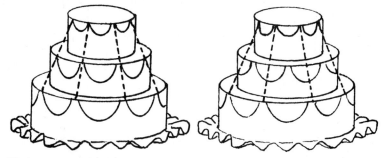

This applies to tiers with or without separators.

6. If two tiers are stacked together without separators, and the lower one is setting on a separator plate, be sure to check location of little legs underneath plate so markings will be in the same place on top edge of tier.

7. When decorating a tier with a separator plate on top, use a small star or round tube and pipe a shell or bulb border around edge of plate before making borders and flower sprays on top edge of tier.

Place damp cloth under plate smaller than turn table to keep from sliding.

8.   When separated tiers are assembled at place of reception, pillars should line up exactly the same on all tiers. The spacing of decorations should also match up with other tiers, whether they are:

(a) the same on each
     tier..............OR....alternated.

9.   Pipe borders and side decorations first, then make the flower sprays.

NOTE: *The designs described in this chapter, using combinations of borders, garlands and flower sprays, are standard designs which have been used over the years. They are presented here only as a basic arrangement of decorations for wedding cakes.*

Many variations of these designs are possible, of course, as well as your own ideas of new, creative designs which you may wish to execute on your wedding cakes. The field is unlimited!

DELIVERING

XI

Transporting the Cake

One of the most important--but often overlooked--aspects in decorating is transportation.

What does it profit you to create a beautiful masterpiece, only to have it defaced or destroyed on the way to the reception?

If the damage is your fault, you'll have to make repairs, or possibly refund some money to the bride (if you can't get the cake back into its original shape). Therefore, take extreme care and caution in delivering your cake.

There's nothing to it....if you'll follow a few simple rules. (Incidentally, you should always consider delivering your cakes rather than having the bride or her family do it, for reasons explained in the chapter on "How to Price Your Cakes".)

CARRY EXTRA ICING

When delivering a cake, always have on hand, extra icing in a bag, and a few flowers so you can repair any damage that may occur. If you're careful, major damage won't happen (barring an automobile accident).

But often, in lifting cakes from the car or from their cartons, the cake might separate slightly from the plate it's on. With the extra icing, you can cover that in a matter of seconds.

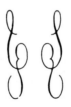

HOW TO BOX A CAKE

WITHOUT SEPARATORS

If your cake does not have separators between the tiers, it must be completely assembled and decorated before being transported. This would, of course, include two or three non-separated tiers that may be part of a larger cake where some of the tiers are separated.

Get some large, clean corrugated cardboard boxes from a grocery or drug store. They do not need tops. If a box is too tall, it should be cut down before cake is placed in it. If box is square and same size as diameter of cake base, cut down two corners of box. Cake can then be slid into open side, then corners taped back together.

If box is larger than cake base, make five or six 1" rolls of wide masking tape, sticky side out. Place on bottom of box underneath where cake will be setting. This should keep it from sliding around inside box.

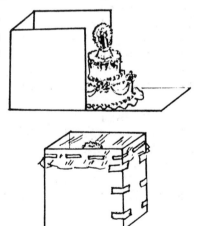

Finally, place plastic wrap over top & tape around sides of box to keep out dust, bugs, etc.

WITH SEPARATORS

Tiers setting on separator plates, (whether one, two or three tiers), should be placed in boxes with foam rubber mats on the bottom. Stick foam rubber down with afore-mentioned rolls of masking tape. This should keep plate legs from sliding. Place each tier, or tiers, with plate in separate box and cover with plastic wrap.

When transporting the cake in a vehicle, make sure the box is setting level and make no sudden stops while driving! It should be setting on a foam rubber mat, whether on seat or floor to cushion shock. When carrying box in your arms, keep it level.

Cake should be placed on the table exactly where it is to be for the reception. Set the bottom tier in place first, then assemble the other tiers on top. A cake with separators should never be moved after assembly, unless it is taken apart completely, then re-assembled at different location.

Be sure to leave a list of items used on cake---plates, pillars, etc.---with bride's mother or someone responsible, so items will be returned to you. Following is a form you might wish to use and/or adapt for this purpose.

DEPOSIT REFUND LIST

FOR _____

WEDDING DATE _____

The following items MUST be returned by DATE _____ for full deposit refund.
After this date, an additional $2.00 per day rental will be charged on stands and
an additional $3.00 per day rental will be charged on Fountains. Items MUST be re-
turned in good condition. Do NOT wash items in HOT water. DO NOT wash Fountains.
This slip MUST be returned along with the items.

PILLARS	NUMBER OF	SEPARATOR PLATES	NUMBER OF	OTHER ITEMS	NUMBER OF
13"	_____	18"	_____	_____	_____
12"	_____	16"	_____	_____	_____
10½"	_____	14"	_____	_____	_____
5"	_____	12"	_____	_____	_____
4"	_____	10"	_____	_____	_____
3"	_____	8"	_____	_____	_____
FOUNTAIN	_____	6"	_____	_____	_____

CUTTING

XII

Cutting the Cake

Having the cake into proper serving-sizes is vitally important, not only for the bride and her guests, but for your reputation as well!

If the person charged with cutting the cake serves too large a piece, your 100-serving cake will <u>not</u> serve 100 people.

While this seems quite obvious, the fact is that untrained people overseeing the reception table often slice cake like a piece of pie--in a large wedge!!

And when the cake runs out before all guests are served, the assumption is that you did not make the cake big enough (while that isn't your fault, you'll hear about it and probably have to defend yourself and your reputation).

If you are not going to be cutting your own creation at the reception table, better make sure the bride, or her mother, knows how it's done so they can instruct their people in the correct method.

And the best way to do this is to have a Cake Cutting Guide like the one reprinted in this chapter. Give it to your customer at the time she orders, or better yet (since they might lose it), deliver it along with the cake on the wedding day.

CAKE CUTTING GUIDE

When cutting a decorated cake, whether it's a small one for a birthday, or for a very large wedding, it is advisable to have on hand, a folded damp towel on a small plate. The cutting knife should be wiped on the towel after every few pieces are cut. For a large cake, the plate and towel should be changed several times during the cutting. A large tray should also be on hand alongside the wedding cake on which to place the separators, plates, dowels, etc. when removed from the cake.

TIERED WEDDING CAKES WITH SEPARATORS

This is probably the best method to cut large tiers with separators.

STEPS   *(Read completely before starting to cut the cake.)*

No. 1   Remove the top tier (Bride and Groom keepsake tier) and set aside.*

No. 2   Remove next tier and place it in front of you.

No. ③   Cut a 2" strip across the cake, starting at one of the edges.

No. ④   Then, cut this 2" strip into 1" wide pieces. This will make serving pieces, each 1" x 2" x 4" (or whatever the depth of tier).

No. ⑤   Cut across the entire cake, one 2" strip at a time, repeating Step No. 4.

No. 6   When finished, remove the next tier and cut it into pieces as in Steps Nos. 3, 4 and 5.

*Be sure to remove top tier from plate after reception so plate can be returned to decorator along with rest of plates, etc.

After cutting each tier, you'll discover there are some pieces around the edges not exactly 1" x 2". These larger triangle shaped pieces, however, are counted in the yields of servings.

Step No. ③
Start here

Step No. ⑤

Then, Step No. ④
Cut into 1" wide strips

CAKE SIZE	SERVINGS
10"......	40 pieces
12"......	60 "
14"......	80 "
16"......	100 "
18"......	130 "
20"......	160 "

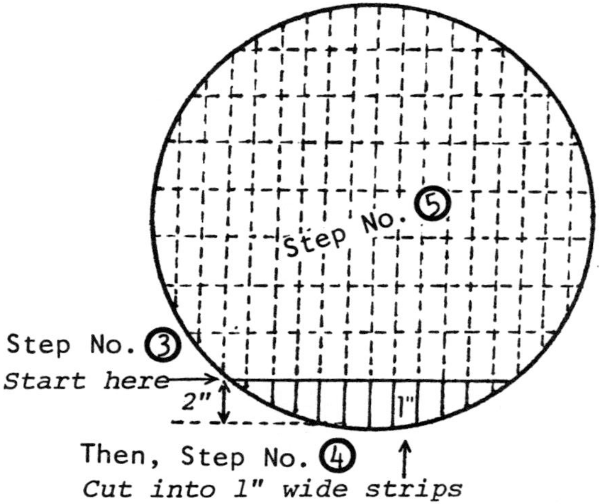

TIERED CAKES WITHOUT SEPARATORS

For smaller tiered cakes without separators,
the following cutting method is possibly the
easiest to use:

1.   Slip point of the knife under the edge
of the cake circle under top tier. Raise
cake up slightly with knife; slip fingertips
of one hand under cake; set knife aside;
slip fingertips of other hand under cake,
then lift straight up. Set cake aside (if
this tier is to be saved for the bride).

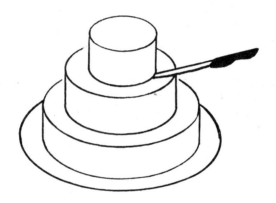

2.   With a sawing up & down motion, cut
around the circle where the top tier was
removed.

3.   Cut slices 1" wide all around the outside ring, then cut 1" slices all around
the center circle.   Remove cake circle.

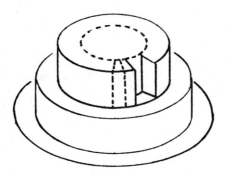

4.   Continue on the bottom tier by cutting
around the cake circle just removed, then
cut 1" slices all around the outside ring.
Cut a smaller circle, then cut 1" slices
from the ring, then slices from the inside
circle.

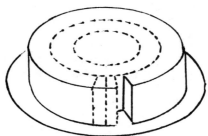

TIERED CAKES WITHOUT SEPARATORS (Cont.)

STACKED TIERS

6"-10" Two Tiered Cake

```
 6" tier..15 pcs..............1¼"x 2"
10" tier-⎰ 6" circle..15 pcs..1¼"x 2"
        ⎱10" ring....30 pcs..1" x 2"
              TOTAL 45 pcs.
```

8"-12" Two Tiered Cake

```
 8" tier..24 pcs..............1" x 3"
12" tier-⎰ 8" circle..24 pcs..1" x 3"
        ⎱12" ring....36 pcs..1" x 2"
              TOTAL 60 pcs.
```

6"-10"-14" Three Tiered Cake

```
 6" tier..15 pcs..............1¼"x 2"
10" tier-⎰ 6" circle..15 pcs..1¼"x 2"
        ⎱10" ring....30 pcs..1" x 2"
         ⎧ 6" circle..15 pcs..1¼" x 2"
14" tier-⎨10" ring....30 pcs..1" x 2"
         ⎩14" ring....42 pcs..1" x 2"
              TOTAL 132 pcs.
```

NOTE: Total pieces for each cake does not include top tier.

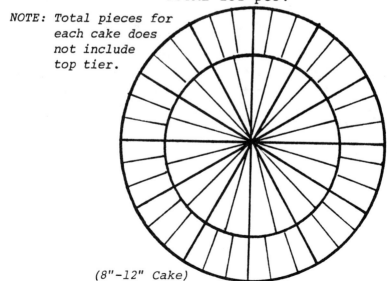

(8"-12" Cake)

TIERED CAKES WITHOUT SEPARATORS (Cont.)

     The method for cutting tiered cakes without separators can also be used for cutting single tiered cakes, such as birthday cakes, etc.* The number of servings listed in the following charts are based on starting each slice approximately 1" apart around the outside of the ring or circle.

For a round single tier cake that is 10" or less, this method is probably the easiest to use.

SINGLE TIER CAKES

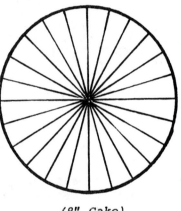

Cake Diam.	No. Pcs.	Size Pcs.
6"	15	1¼"x 2"
7"	20	1"x 2½"
8"	24	1"x 3"
9"	28	1"x 3½"
10"	30	1"x 4"

(8" Cake)

(When cutting a cake into wedge type slices, a circle of about 2" in the center is not counted in the size of the slices, since this portion most likely will be crumbs or too thin to be considered a part of the slice.)

SQUARE & UNUSUAL SHAPED TIERED CAKES

Square cakes are probably
the easiest of all tiered
cakes to cut. Use method
on Pages 100-101 for "Tiered
Cakes with Separators" for
cutting squares. Method
shown on Pages 103 & 104 may
be used for cutting square
cakes <u>without</u> separators
if there <u>is</u> at least four
inches difference in sizes of tiers.

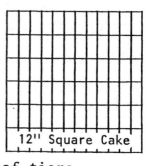

12" Square Cake

Heart, Petal & Hexagon shaped cakes are
also cut by the method on Pages 100 & 101
If no separators are used between tiers on
these cakes, tiers must be lifted off and
cut by same method.

SHEET CAKES

Oftentimes, sheet cakes are
made to accompany wedding
cakes. They can be square
or rectangular and are
usually marked off (but not
cut) into servings and each
piece decorated to match
the wedding cake.

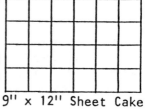

9" x 12" Sheet Cake

For example, if the cake is decorated with
roses, each piece of sheet cake would have
a small rosebud in matching colors.

To mark a square or rectangular cake into
particular sized servings, use a ruler or
yardstick and make little marks with a
toothpick around all four sides at each
place where the cake is to be cut.

In other words, if the servings are to be 2" x 2" square, mark every two inches on all four sides of the cake. If the servings are to be 1" x 2", mark every two inches on two opposite sides of the cake and every inch on other two sides.

To make lines between the markings over the whole cake: On smaller cakes, it is rather simple to use the point of a cutting knife to scratch a line across the cake from marking to marking. For a very large sheet cake, use a piece of thread as long as the widest side of the cake, hold it taut, line it up with parallel markings on each side of cake, then lower it down slightly into surface of icing. Move the thread just a tiny bit in one direction, then lift up from cake. Repeat this between all markings.

In regard to the size of the servings that a square or rectangular cake may yield: for a one-layer, 2" squares are probably the most popular. Thus, if you have a 9" x 12" cake, the 9" sides should be marked into 2 1/4" spaces and the 12" sides, into 2" spaces. Admittedly, these would be slightly larger than the 2" x 2" size, but would be the only logical way to divide the cake. If the cake is a two-layer, then the pieces could be 1" x 2" and be marked into 1" spaces on the 9" sides and 2" spaces on the 12" sides. The one-layer would yield 24 pieces and the two-layer, 54 pieces. This same method of figuring applies to any size square or rectangular cake.

XIII

There's BIG MONEY in Cake Decorating

This section has been written for the Cake Decorator who wants to earn extra income from this marvelous art.

And there is a lot of money to be made selling Decorated Cakes.

In fact, what follows in the next two chapters on "Pricing Your Cakes" and "Advertising" are <u>very</u> <u>condensed</u> excerpts from the popular book, "How to Make Money in Cake Decorating: Owning & Operating a Successful Business in Your Home".

A home business is an excellent way to provide a supplemental income for you and your family---and still stay around the house if you have children in need of supervision.

In this day of traumatic economic conditions, a home business is simply a fantastic way to fight back to get those little "extra" things that make life pleasant and necessary, the "extras" that many other people have to forego because of inflation.

The Baked Foods business is one of the few businesses that are virtually recession proof. People will cut back on buying that new car. They will eat ground beef instead of steak. They will wear last year's clothes instead of today's fashions.

But it's a proven fact that weddings are not canceled because of bad times, and parties--birthday, office, retirement, showers, anniversaries--still go on because there are just certain things that people will not deny themselves. If nothing else, they view these celebrations - complete with decorated cakes - as bright spots in an otherwise bleak routine!

There are tens of thousands of people today who've made a full-time career--and considerable money--from decorating cakes. Many are still working from their homes, while others have started their own independent stores and bakeries.

The field is still wide-open!

YOU CAN BE LIKE GENERAL MOTORS

A full-time, or even a part-time business--- operated like a business (and not like a hobby)---can use the same tax advantages-- or tax shelters--as do the largest corporations in the country----General Motors, IBM, Exxon Oil, Coca Cola, etc.

And it makes no difference that you are operating from home. A business needn't necessarily be in a separate store or in a shopping center to qualify for tax advantages.

In "How to Make Money in Cake Decorating", the author goes into great detail, not only on Pricing and Advertising (much more than is offered in the next chapters), but also in all aspects of starting a decorating business, such as:

The importance of choosing an effective name; getting licenses (if needed); proper bookkeeping; how to diversify into profit- able sidelines; great tax savings; the best-- and worst--kinds of advertising; dozens of money-making secrets; and Much, Much More!

This is absolutely the first book ever to deal exclusively with the business-side of Cake Decorating.

While "How to Make Money in Cake Deco- rating" has been written for the beginner in business, it will also greatly benefit those who already have their own business, and are looking for valuable and labor-sav- ing pointers, and new money making ideas!

All the methods in the book have proven successful to others.

The book tells you exactly:

- How to start out easily and simply.
- How to determine the investment needed (not much).
- How to spend the least money for supplies and ingredients.
- How to get inexpensive printing.
- How to get a fair price for your cakes (and how not to underprice them).

- How to start a Related Business and make even more money!
- How to Save money with "Penny Pinching" ideas.
- How to do your own inexpensive promotion and advertising.
- What kind of Advertising to avoid.
- How to handle customers successfully.
- How to get every tax deduction possible.
- How to keep records

and more!

If you've been thinking about a business of your own---or if you currently have a business or operate a bakery shoppe---then you shouldn't be without "How to Make Money in Cake Decorating". There are many methods even the most experienced baker/decorator will find of value.

And although there are dozens of money-making ideas, the chapter on Tax Deductions alone could save you much more than the cost of the book (which is only ($9.95).

For a copy of this book, check with your local Cake Decorating Supply store or your favorite mail order source.

If not available from those places, write Deco-Press for information where you may obtain this book.

Now...on to "Pricing" and "Advertising"...

XIV

How to Price Your Cakes

There are a number of ways to establish prices.

First--and foremost--find out what the competition is charging. As a beginner, you can ill afford to charge more than established bakeries and independent decorators.

If there is no one in your community doing cakes, your job is a little harder in setting a price. But then you'll have the field all to yourself! Oh, to be so lucky!

If you're a total beginner, you'll not know whether to charge $25 for a 100-serving cake, or $100!

Study the Sample Price List on the following page. This will serve as a guide and give you an idea, at least. Keep in mind this list is for Denver, Colorado and may not be appropriate for your town. *(Prices were in effect at time of publication.)*

WEDDING CAKE PRICES

Except for very detailed and/or elaborate cake styles, all prices below are based upon the number of servings requested.

(Prices do not include an ornament)

Servings	Price	Servings	Price
25	$ 44.75	250	$233.50
50	62.00	275	260.50
75	111.85	300	271.75
100	127.50	325	312.50
125	139.75	350	326.00
150	149.75	375	342.50
175	165.50	400	413.50
200	186.50	450	485.50
225	206.50	500	593.00

The number of above servings is based on a piece of cake 1"x 2"x depth (3 or 4 inches). If you wish to serve a larger piece of cake, you should order a larger size cake to accommodate this.

SHEET CAKES

(One layer, approx. 1½" deep.)

Servings	Price
24	$16.50
48	24.00
96	34.00

Sheet cakes are marked to be cut 2" x 2".

(Prices subject to change without notice.)

KNOWING YOUR COSTS

Setting a price on your wedding cakes is simply a matter of knowing the cost of your ingredients and materials (batter, icing, cake circles, doilies, ruffle, etc.) plus the time it takes you to do everything, right up to the delivery (time required to do one-tiered special occasion cakes should give you a basis for figuring this, just as the charts on how much batter and icing will help you determine the cost of materials).

Your ingredient and material costs should be doubled or tripled, at least. Whether you wish merely to make the prevailing minimum wage for your time, or set a higher price for your talent and know-how, is up to you. Don't give your time and talent away. But don't price yourself out of the market, either.

WEDDING ORNAMENTS

Cake ornaments are not normally included in the price of your cake. This is an extra charge for the bride if she gets it from you. Some brides buy tops elsewhere.

DEPOSITS

Always charge a "stand" deposit for the separator plates, pillars, cake plates, etc. you send out with the cake. Otherwise, you'll soon discover how often these items are not returned. And that means profit wiped out by your having to purchase replacement items.

As well intentioned and honest as your customer might be, it is simply too easy for them to "overlook" or "forget" to return plates and pillars. If they've got money on deposit to be refunded, they'll make the return! If they don't, you have their money to replace the stands.

A deposit also allows you to deduct from it any item that was broken or lost by the customer.

A stand deposit should also be non-refundable if customer cancels her cake beyond a certain deadline, say 10 days prior to the delivery date. What if you've got flowers all made up and the cake ready to go into the oven, and you learn customer is cancelling out? You should not have to lose money on it.

If, however, a customer cancels more than 10 days ahead (or whatever you feel is right), you should refund the deposit.

FOUNTAIN RENTALS

To increase your profits, consider having a water fountain to rent with your cakes. If a bride gets her cake from you, the rental fee should be $5 up, plus a hefty deposit to cover its loss or damage (as fountains are more fragile than plates and pillars).

If someone merely wants to rent the fountain (but not get a cake), you can charge from $15 to $20 for the weekend, plus a deposit.

DELIVERY

Delivering cakes is essential for two reasons: (1) for the customer's convenience and (2) to protect your reputation.

Most customers aren't competent to deliver the cake, much less set it up at the reception. And if your cake is damaged in transit or in trying to be set up by others, your reputation will suffer.

It is the rare customer who'll tell their guests that the condition of the cake is "my fault". People will look at it and assume you--the decorator--did a lousy job. How many future sales will you get from that bad looking cake?

You can either charge (1) a delivery and set-up fee, in addition to the price of the cake, or (2) have it included in the established price you quote to people.

XV

Advertising

for Little or No Money

Whether you're just starting to sell Wedding Cakes or have been at it for some time, you should know about advertising.

Everyone has <u>heard</u> about advertising... but few people really <u>know</u> about it.

There are many ways to advertise. And you can spend as little or as much as you wish.

Since cake decorators working from home have little to spend on advertising, we shall tell you of the "inexpensive" ways to get your message to the public.

The cheapest-- and most effective form of advertising--is:

WORD OF MOUTH

If you put out a good product and your service is excellent, the "word of mouth" will get around, and your business will expand and grow. And it will have cost you nothing "extra". (Conversely, a lousy product and poor service will make the "word" spread even faster to stay away from you.)

BUSINESS CARDS

In the "paid advertising" category, the first thing you should consider is--- Business Cards---those little 2" x 3" white cards with your name, address and phone number. You can get them from your local printer.

Every chance you get, pass out the cards... to friends, relatives, old customers, new customers, strangers. Put one in each cake order. Tack them on community bulletin boards. Put some on the reception table by your beautiful creation. Ask other people to hand them out for you.

Business cards are one of the least expensive advertising items you'll find.

CLASSIFIED ADVERTISING

A fairly inexpensive method is the classified ad section of the newspapers. Rates are usually quoted in the classified section itself. If not, call the paper and ask their rates.

There are two categories of newspapers--- paid subscriptions and free (or "throw-a-ways"). Paid subscriptions are published either daily or weekly, while throw-a-ways are put out weekly or monthly.

You'll pay a great deal more for ads in the daily newspaper than for the free paper, but in most cases, the paid paper is more effective.

Don't expect to run one or two small classified ads and have them be effective. You'll only waste your money.

Figure out what you can spend over a given time--say two or three months--and then compose an ad and let it run. See what results you get.

Advertise in your church paper or calendar, if they have one. It's usually pretty cheap, but does have a limited audience.

Many civic and fraternal organizations have papers, bulletins, calendars, newsletters that take paid advertising. Check out these sources--like the Shriners, Knights of Columbus, professional sororities, etc.

Here is just one example of a classified ad you might run:

```
┌─────────────────────────────────────────────┐
│        WEDDING CAKES MADE-TO-ORDER           │
│                                              │
│ Delicious Cakes for Weddings, Birthdays and  │
│ all other occasions.  Beautifully decorated. │
│            Special Order Only.               │
│ Call The Cake Lady          Phone 123-4567   │
└─────────────────────────────────────────────┘
```

RADIO-TV

We do not suggest this medium for the small volume decorator. It is simply too expensive, and unless you're prepared to spend a great deal of money, Radio-TV is not effective.

SIGNS

Consider magnetic signs for your car. These are plastic products and are relatively cheap. They can be very effective in keeping your name before the public.

They can be put on your car easily and removed easily without harm to the car's finish.

If you don't wish to drive with your sign always on the car, make sure it's on there when you deliver cakes, so people coming to the reception can see it.

Also inexpensive is a small sign (about 5"x 7") to leave by your cake on the reception table. "This cake created by The Cake Lady", along with a phone number. The sign should not be obtrusive or take away from the reception table and cake. If you are creative enough to letter your own sign, fine. But don't put something by the cake which looks amateurish and "home made". In that case, get a professional sign painter. You should also ask the bride's permission to do this (and then be sure to pick up the sign later).

DEMONSTRATIONS

Give cake decorating demonstrations for various clubs, groups, organizations. Nothing draws more "oohs" and "aahs" from a crowd than seeing a masterpiece created right in front of its eyes!

PRICE LIST AND CATALOGUE

You can prepare a price list about as inexpensive as Business Cards. It need not be elaborate (but don't do it haphazardly).

If you have a good typewriter, follow the style of the Price List on Page 116, take it to a Quick Printer and have them run off as many copies as you need. Or if you have access to a good mimeograph machine, you can do it yourself.

You definitely should have some kind of catalogue or pictures to show customers, or at the very least, decorated dummy cakes on display.

If you don't have color photographs of the cakes you've actually done, cut out pictures from the many cake decorating books available from Wilton and other sources. Put them in plastic covers in a photo album. (If you do this, make sure you can deliver a cake exactly as shown in the pictures, or your customers may be a bit disappointed.)

You may not be able to afford beautiful, professionally done photos of your cakes, but in today's Polaroid World--it should not be an expensive proposition to take your own.

Wedding Anniversaries

If you are decorating a cake for a wedding anniversary, the following listings may be useful in planning the whole celebration, including appropriate flowers for the cake and gifts for specific anniversaries.

◼ ◼ ◼ GIFTS ◼ ◼ ◼

	Traditional	*Modern*
First	Paper	Clocks
Second	Cotton	China
Third	Leather	Crystal, Glass
Fourth	Books	Appliances
Fifth	Wood	Silverware
Sixth	Iron	Wood
Seventh	Copper, Bronze	Desk Sets
Eighth	Appliances	Linens & Laces
Ninth	Pottery	Leather
Tenth	Tin, Aluminum	Diamond Jewelry
Eleventh	Steel	Fashion Jewelry
Twelfth	Silk, Linen	Pearls
Thirteenth	Lace	Textiles, Furs
Fourteenth	Ivory	Gold Jewelry
Fifteenth	Crystal	Watches
Sixteenth		Silver Flatware
Seventeenth		Furniture
Eighteenth		Porcelain
Nineteenth		Bronze
Twentieth	China	Platinum
Twenty-Fifth	Silver	Sterling Silver
Thirtieth	Pearl	Diamond
Thirty-Fifth	Coral	Jade
Fortieth	Ruby	Ruby
Forty-Fifth	Sapphire	Sapphire
Fiftieth	Gold	Gold
Fifty-Fifth	Emerald	Emerald
Sixtieth	Diamond	Diamond

Anniversaries over Sixtieth are celebrated as Diamond Jubilees.

FLOWERS FOR EACH MONTH

January........Snowdrop--Carnation
February.......Violet--Primrose
March..........Jonquil--Daffodil
April..........Daisy--Sweet Pea
May............Lily of the Valley--Hawthorne
June...........Rose--Honeysuckle
July...........Larkspur--Water Lily
August.........Poppy--Gladiola
September......Morning Glory--Astor
October........Calendula--Cosmos
November.......Chrysanthemum
December.......Narcissus

JEWELS FOR EACH MONTH

January...........Garnet
February..........Amethyst
March.............Aquamarine
April.............Diamond
May...............Emerald
June..............Pearl
July..............Ruby
August............Sardonyx
September.........Sapphire
October...........Opal
November..........Topaz
December..........Turquoise

Percent of Marriages Per Month

Based on a national 5-year Average, the following statistics show what percentage of marriages takes place each month.

Does it surprise you to learn that June is NOT the biggest Wedding Month? Currently, June ranks second.

For the reader in the business of Wedding Cakes, the information should help you better plan your merchandising and advertising/promotion activities.

1.	August	12%
2.	June	11.3%
3.	July	9%
4.	May	8.8%
	September (tied)	8.8%
5.	December	8.4%
6.	October	8%
7.	November	7.9%
8.	April	7%
9.	March	6.6%
10.	February	6.5%
11.	January	5.7%

Questions & Answers

The following represent questions Esther Murphy has answered over her long and distinguished career.

Question: *My Wedding Cake seems to have a lot of large holes after I bake it. It's just too porous. Can you help me?*

Answer: A couple of things might have happened. You may have beaten the batter too much, or baked it at too high a temperature. To get rid of the air holes, hold the pans about 6 inches from the top of the table, and drop them. Do this several times to each pan. The bubbles making the holes will rise to the top and disappear. Thus, after the baking is over, your cakes should have a fine texture WITHOUT HOLES.

Question: *How do you get icing to stick to a cake that has been sliced?*

Answer: Using a spatula to apply icing to a cut portion of a cake tends to pull crumbs off instead of leaving icing on. To remedy this, apply your icing with a tube first, THEN smooth it over with a spatula.

Question: *My cakes have a tendency to break when I dump them after baking. Any suggestions how to fix them when this happens?*

Answer: The remedy is similar to the question above: Squeeze icing onto the broken portions using a tube directly against the cake (not a spatula). The icing is forced into the pores and when pressed together, the broken pieces will stick. (Whoever gets the servings from these pieces will get more.icing!!)

Question: *My cakes seem hopelessly lopsided after baking. Is there a remedy for this?*

Answer: If there is a hump in the center of the cake, merely slice it off with a long serrated knife. If one side is higher that the other, slice off that side, and then spread icing on the lower side, and place the piece of cut-off cake onto the new icing.

Question: *What do you do to a large cake that is sunken and soggy in the center after baking?*

Answer: Cut a circle out of the center. Then cut the same size circle out of a smaller cake and insert it into the hole in the large cake., using the same method for sticking together as used for the broken cake.

Question: *My icing often is too stiff to apply smoothly. What should I do?*

Answer: Add whatever liquid is called for in your recipe and re-beat at low speed.

Question: *My icing is too porous. How can I solve that?*

Answer: To get rid of all those air bubbles in your icing, stir with a wide spatula, or rebeat the icing at low speed for several minutes on your mixer.

Question: *Whenever I pick up or move some of my large wedding cakes, the icing cracks. What's wrong?*

Answer: The base is too flexible. To prevent these kinds of cracks, on large cakes, you must use a sturdy base, either made from plastic, plywood or masonite.

About the Author

Esther Murphy is one of the pioneers of American Cake Decorating. Long before the current crop of books appeared on the scene, Esther wrote and illustrated the two best-selling decorating books of the day---- "The Art of Creative Cake Decorating" and "Holiday and Party Cakes".

Although those publications are out of print today, they have become collector's items, much sought after by decorators.

Many successful and talented cake decorators throughout the country today are either former students of Esther's or cut their decorating teeth on her books. She is known and admired by thou- sands of decorators.

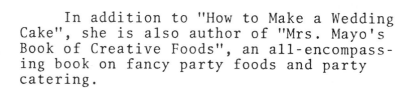

Since the early 1970's, she has been chief designer and teacher for the Mrs. Mayo's Company.

In addition to "How to Make a Wedding Cake", she is also author of "Mrs. Mayo's Book of Creative Foods", an all-encompass- ing book on fancy party foods and party catering.

INDEX

- A -

Advertising
    Business Cards, 124
    Catalogue, 127
    Classified ads, 124, 125
    Demonstrations, 127
    Price lists, 127
    Radio, 125
    Television, 125
    Signs, 125, 126
    Word-of-mouth, 123

Assembling the Cake
    Crystal Clear Dividers, 74, 75
    Fountain Cake, 76, 77, 78
    Lace Cake Stand, 70, 71, 72
    (with 4-Arm Support), 73
    Tiers
        Not separated, 15, 67, 83
        Round Cakes, 19
        Separated, 14, 67, 83

        Tiering Techniques, 65, 66, 67, 68,
                69, 70, 71, 72, 73, 74, 75,
                76, 77, 78, 83, 84, 85, 86

- B -

Baking, 35
    High Altitude, 39
    Times, 38, 39
    Tips for, 36, 37
    Temperatures, 38, 39

Designs, proper, 12, 83, 84, 85
Dumping the Cake, 43, 44

- F -

Fillings, 60
Flowers, 130
Fountain Cakes, 76, 77, 78
Fountain Rentals, 118
Freezing Cakes, 37

- H -

High Altitude, 32, 39

- I -

Icing, 47
    Amount needed, Round Cakes, 55
    Amount needed, Sheet Cakes, 56
    Amount needed, Square Cakes, 55
    Buttercream, 48
    Chocolate Buttercream, 49
    Royal, 50, 51

Icing the Cake
    Techniques, 59, 60, 61, 62

- J -

Jewels, 130

Signs, 125

- T -

Television, 125
Temperatures, 38, 39
Tiers,
    Crystal Clear Dividers, 74, 75
    Fountain Cake, 76, 77, 78
    Lace Cake Stand, 70, 71, 72
        With 4-Arm Support, 73

Tier Assembly (see ASSEMBLING THE CAKE)
Transporting the Cake (see DELIVERY)

- V -

Vanilla, White (clear), 13, 29, 47, 48

- W -

Wedding Anniversaries, 129